PRAISE FOR

THE PLAYBOOK

FROM BIG-TIME PLAYERS

"*The Playbook* is an American import I can wholeheartedly endorse!"

> —Fidel Castro, former dictat— prime min— presid—
> the dude with the cigar and the silly painter hat

"If I were alive today and could read English, *The Playbook* would be on my nightstand for sure. Thanks, Barney!"

> —Genghis Khan, Mongol warrior and suspected genetic father
> of .25% of the human race (that would be a *great*
> Maury episode, b-t-dub)

"There are over 13,000 reasons to buy *The Playbook*."

> —Warren Beatty, Hollywood/bedroom legend

"You want me to endorse what? Where is everybody? This *is* a fund-raiser for my African economic development initiative, right?"

> —Bill Clinton, former United States president

ALSO BY BARNEY STINSON

THE BRO CODE

BRO ON THE GO

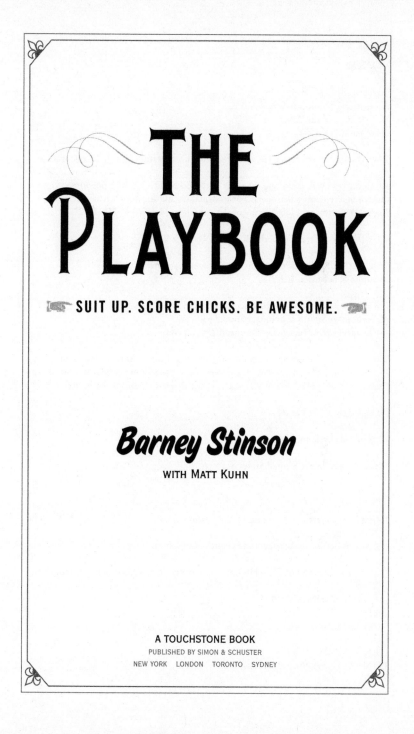

THE PLAYBOOK

SUIT UP. SCORE CHICKS. BE AWESOME.

Barney Stinson

WITH MATT KUHN

A TOUCHSTONE BOOK

PUBLISHED BY SIMON & SCHUSTER

NEW YORK   LONDON   TORONTO   SYDNEY

Touchstone
A Division of Simon & Schuster, Inc.
1230 Avenue of the Americas
New York, NY 10020

First Touchstone trade paperback edition October 2010

TOUCHSTONE and colophon are registered trademarks
of Simon & Schuster, Inc.

For information about special discounts for bulk purchases,
please contact Simon & Schuster Special Sales at
1-800-456-6798 or business@simonandschuster.com.

The Simon & Schuster Speakers Bureau can bring authors to your live event.
For more information or to book an event contact the Simon & Schuster Speakers
Bureau at 1-866-248-3049 or visit our website at www.simonspeakers.com.

Designed by Ruth Lee-Mui

Illustrations by Jenni Hendriks

Manufactured in the United States of America

20 19

Library of Congress Cataloging-in-Publication Data
    Kuhn, Matt.
    The playbook / by Barney Stinson with Matt Kuhn.
        p. cm.
        1. Men—Conduct of life—Humor.   2. Dating (Social customs)—Humor.
I. Title.
    PN6231.M45K854 2009
    818'.602—dc22
                        2010024803

ISBN 978-1-4391-9683-0
ISBN 978-1-4391-9905-3 (ebook)

The Playbook *is dedicated to*
those beautiful creatures that can make
a young boy's heart leap,
a middle-aged man weep with joy,
and an old man smile:
boobs.

You can discover more about a person in an hour of play than in a year of conversation.

—Plato

CONTENTS

INTRODUCTION

First of all, thanks for purchasing this book! Now, if you're reading this, I'm guessing you're either too pathetic to pick up girls on your own, or you're looking for some creative ideas to spice up your repertoire—but my money's on "too pathetic to pick up girls on your own."

You stumble up to a woman and stammer in a rehearsed yet cracking voice, "Can I get your number?" Your trembling hands are stuffed in your pockets in a futile attempt to look cool. You're dressed like an overgrown eighth grader. You're a little out of shape. Geez, buddy, you're kind of a mess, huh? Ooh, I bet you smell too.

The good news is you're not alone, Ted. There are millions of unattractive chumps just like you all over the place who apparently never want to sleep with a woman. But all of that is going to change because now, with the help of *The Playbook,* you'll be able to approach any beautiful woman you want and trick her into sleeping with you. How? By giving you self-confidence and proving that you really are somebody who matters (even though you're not).

Again, sincerely, thanks for purchasing this book.

WHAT IS *THE PLAYBOOK*?

*T**he Playbook* provides a plenitude of plays to profit the per-sistent player. Contained within these pages are every scam, con, hustle, hoodwink, gambit, flimflam, stratagem, and bamboozle I've ever used or ever hope to use to pick up chicks and give them the business. Now, in an act of selfless charity, I'm passing this treasure of pleasure on to you as an easy-to-follow guide.

Included in this collection are more than seventy-five schemes that are guaranteed to attract all kinds of women, no matter how sorrowful your social skills are. Best of all, most of the plays re-quire no experience and little to no preparation, so you have almost everything you need to get started right away. Almost: 83% of the plays will necessitate at least a few yards of aluminum foil, so before you get cracking you'd be wise to buy in bulk at your local big-box store or discount warehouse retailer.

With so many other pickup programs available on the market today, you might be wondering what makes *The Playbook* unique. First of all, I created this program, so you know it's gonna be awe-some. Second, I've slept with enough hotties to overbook a com-mercial airliner (several of them *on* a commercial airliner, what up?) and only once had to wear eyeliner and a goofy hat to do it . . . and that was only because this chick had been in a coma since 1983 and pretending to be Boy George was such an obvious layup.

Last, and most important, other seduction methods preach "social dynamics" in which you insult women in an attempt to attract them. I find that approach both demeaning and offensive. Rather than degrade women, *The Playbook* centers on the profound, positive, and personal changes *you* can make to trick hot sluts into sleeping with you.

HOW DOES
THE PLAYBOOK WORK?

The plays in this book are scientifically calibrated to excite the female sex nodes enough to make her actually consider having sex with a stranger. This strategy flies in the face of conventional wisdom, because for countless millennia men were led to believe that women were not interested in casual sex. We were told their libido had been replaced with the urge to have children, make dinner, and discover the planet's cutest handbag. But recent evidence suggests that women enjoy sex almost as much as finding a Christian Dior clutch in white croc at 30% off.

Now, thanks to science, we can generate a clearer picture of what women are looking for in a sexual partner. After years of in-depth field research (*very* in-depth), I've discovered that women are sexually aroused by four primary factors:

1. Money
2. Fame
3. Vulnerability
4. Emotional and spiritual fulfillment

Obviously, number four is right out the window. Seducing a woman by satisfying her on an emotional level is difficult, time-consuming, and quite frankly, unrewarding.

Therefore *The Playbook* focuses on transforming you into someone who reflects some or all of those first three qualities. If you're wondering why you have to change who you are, consider this: is a woman more likely to sleep with a loser like you or an underwater bomb diffuser who grew up in an orphanage? It's just science.

Using all this information, here's a composite sketch of what women might consider the most sexually attractive man ever.

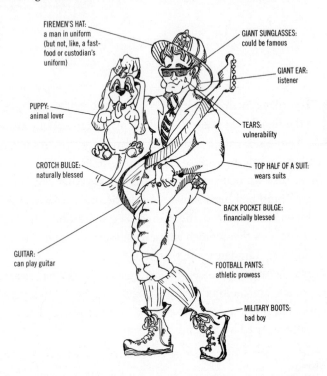

FIREMEN'S HAT:
a man in uniform
(but not, like, a fast-
food or custodian's
uniform)

GIANT SUNGLASSES:
could be famous

GIANT EAR:
listener

PUPPY:
animal lover

TEARS:
vulnerability

CROTCH BULGE:
naturally blessed

TOP HALF OF A SUIT:
wears suits

BACK POCKET BULGE:
financially blessed

GUITAR:
can play guitar

FOOTBALL PANTS:
athletic prowess

MILITARY BOOTS:
bad boy

Don't worry, *The Playbook* will never ask you to dress up like this bozo. You'll be asked to dress up like a fireman or a football player but never at the same time.

HOW TO USE
THE PLAYBOOK

As you flip through *The Playbook* you'll notice that each play is presented in an easy-to-follow recipe format. This is done so that even a chump like you has a shot at glory. Immediately following the title of the play is a profile box that presents the following quick reference information:

Success Rate—the likelihood of "completing" the play
Attracts—the type of chick the play is designed to ensnare
Requirements—the props and/or special talents you'll need
Prep Time—how much time you need to invest in the play
Bummers—potential negatives to running the play, other than "might totally fail"

Following the profile box are the numbered steps for each play. Simply follow them word for word with absolutely no deviation and you'll get laid. Maybe.

Now, before you flip to a page and start trying out plays on random chicks, there are three things you need to consider.

1. LOCATION. LOCATION. LOCATION.

While most plays can be performed at a party or in your local bar, I recommend you workshop these plays elsewhere when you're just getting your feet wet—if you have any hope of getting other areas wet. Beta-testing a play in a foreign environment safeguards you from any emotional damage, physical harm, or heaven forbid, your bros giving you crap for striking out.

2. MAD PROPS

Some of the plays entail wardrobe elements or other accessories that might not be readily available about the home. Therefore it's a good idea to establish a relationship with a local party or costume shop owner. A good one will let you sample their wares at little to no cost if you promise to promptly return them. As a show of appreciation and good faith you should take extra care not to damage the costume, even as you're climbing out the window of a girl you just duped into sleeping with you. It's called integrity.

3. SKILL LEVEL

Some of the plays require a considerable amount of game while others entail almost no effort whatsoever . . . like The Michael Jordan or The Saudi Prince. *The Playbook* presents plays in increasing order of difficulty so that you can take baby steps on your way to baby-making steps™. This is done for safety. If you tried to run an advanced play like The Land Mine Whisperer without the proper experience, you could wind up seriously hurting your chances of getting laid. It's important to identify your skill level before getting started. That's why I've included the following ASS Test, or Aptitudinal Seduction Skills Test.

ASS TEST
(APTITUDINAL SEDUCTION SKILLS TEST)

Answer the following five questions and then use the secret decoder table to determine your player level.

1. What's the first thing you say to a chick?
   A. "I'm awesome."
   B. "Hi. How are you?"
   C. "Gahhhhhhhhhhhhhhhhhhh!"

2. When you go out, you usually wear
   A. a suit. Duh.
   B. a shirt with a collar, designer denim, dressy shoes—nothing too fancy.
   C. Cheetos-stained jeans, sandals, and a hysterically ironic screen-print T-shirt.

3. A woman's coming over to your place. You
   A. quickly usher the chick from last night off the premises.
   B. scramble to clean up the place and hide any porn.
   C. ask your parents to seriously respect the No Trespassing sign on your door this time.

4. How many ladies have you been with?
   A. please.
   B. I'd rather not say.
   C. probably, like, a million.

5. In the above picture, you are most likely
   A. chatting up that fine illustration of a chick.
   B. sitting with your bros debating which ladies to approach and how—a process that will continue until last call, when you skulk home sad and alone.
   C. not pictured. You were going to go out with your bros but got caught up in an epic World of Warcraft PvP with some kid in Korea... and you totally would have pwned that noob with just a Vindicator's Brand (Mongoose enchant) if the server hadn't crashed.

PLAYER LEVEL

Give yourself 5 points for every A, 3 points for every B, and 1 point for every C.

POINTS	SKILL LEVEL
23–25	Don Juan
16–22	Don Johnson
10–15	Don King
5–9	Don Knotts

THE HISTORY OF
THE PLAYBOOK

Wwhile the collection of plays presented here hails from the incomparable mind of Barney Stinson, it is by no means a new endeavor. In fact, devising schemes to seduce women has been man's primary occupation since before the dawn of history. The proof exists in prehistoric cave paintings.

Cavemen would return home from a hunt carrying one of their buddies, Urk, on their shoulders. They would describe through spirited reenactment what a "dangerous" kill it was and how Urk bravely climbed atop the saber-toothed tiger or mastodon or triceratops or whatever. To help sell the story, they drew pictures of the event on the wall using charcoal and ochre.

Thanks to his bros, Urk would score some major cave tail that night while the others played "rock rock rock" to decide who would be the next day's hero (Urk became ineligible for a week). On the next hunt the men would quickly kill an animal and then spend the rest of the day choreographing the big reenactment and arguing over which cave chicks would look the best clothed. Creating the myth of the all-day hunt served two purposes for cavemen:

it got one guy some easy action and got the rest out of a full day of gathering and nagging.

While The Hero of the Hunt is as old as The I Discovered Fire, it's actually not the oldest trick in the book. That would be The I Love You—which of course had an extra level of complexity before the invention of language.

Surprisingly, the next attempt to record plays didn't occur until the thirteenth century, when monks spent their entire lives writing down seduction scenarios in collections called illuminated manuscripts. Tragically, they were all destroyed by a gaggle of angry nuns.

But, Barney, why would monks spend their entire lives scheming up ways to sleep with women when they had taken a vow of celibacy?

I think you just answered your own question, fake reader.

🐟 FAMOUS PLAYS THROUGHOUT HISTORY 🐟

PLAY	PLAYER	YEAR	HOW IT WORKED
The Royal Burial	King Tut	1323 BC	"Dies" young and is entombed with tons of gold: the original chick magnet.
The Great Last Name	Alexander the Great	325 BC	Conquers much of the known world, creating a legion of angry fathers in order to become the ultimate "bad boy."
The Quetzalcoatl	Hernán Cortés	1519	Convinces women of the Aztec Empire that he's a god by showing them his shiny helmet.
The Insignificant Human	Galileo Galilei	1610	Points his telescope heavenward, proving to chicks how infinitesimal we are, so why not bang?
The Great Compromise	Roger Sherman	1787	Develops the bicameral system of representation to balance power between large and small states but, more important, triple the number of hot young staffers introduced to Washington, DC, every election cycle.
The Me Complex	Napoleon	1811	Generates sympathy among countless European chicks by convincing them he conquered half the continent because he's ashamed of his height.

(*continued on next page*)

PLAY	PLAYER	YEAR	HOW IT WORKED
The Spirit of St. Louis	Charles Lindbergh	1927	Fools the world into thinking flying is dangerous, thereby creating generations of nervous and vulnerable female passengers. Posthumously named president of the mile-high club.
The Gandhi	Mahatma Gandhi	1932	Shaves head, puts on glasses, and goes on a hunger strike to protest something or other. The move reappears half a century later with The Bono.
The Eagle Has Landed	Neil Armstrong	1969	Gets millions of chicks to believe he actually went to the moon— and *walked* on it! Classic.
The I'm George Clooney	George Clooney	1997	Becomes a handsome movie star.

BARNEDICTION

Take a knee, boys.

As we embark on this new mission together, remember *The Playbook* is only a guide. I encourage you to add your own personality and creativity to each and every play. As a wise man once said, it's not the destination but the journey. I think you'll agree in this instance the destination far outweighs the journey, but that doesn't mean you shouldn't try to have fun in the process.

During your adventures you may start to feel the urge to develop your own plays. I highly encourage you to do so, and then post them to barneysblog.com. We should exist as a community of players that can learn and grow from one another's experiences. If you find a new way to get laid, believe me, I'm interested, and will totally *not* steal it and take credit for it in *The Playbook 2*, also by Barney Stinson.

One final note. Throughout your quest you may find yourself mired in a slump, when none of the plays seem to work and you suddenly feel like the worthless individual you were before reading *The Playbook*. That's okay, because while you'll never be as awesome as me, you can rest easy knowing salvation may lie in the very next play. That's the beauty of *The Playbook*—each and every page delivers a new hope that you can trick a girl into having sex with you. Unless it's the last page. Then you're pretty much screwed. Until I write my next book.

—BARNEY STINSON

DISCLAIMER

While each of the plays presented in this book will put you in the best possible position to score, the publisher makes no guarantee you actually will. As the old saying goes, you can lead a horse to water but can't make him have sex with it.

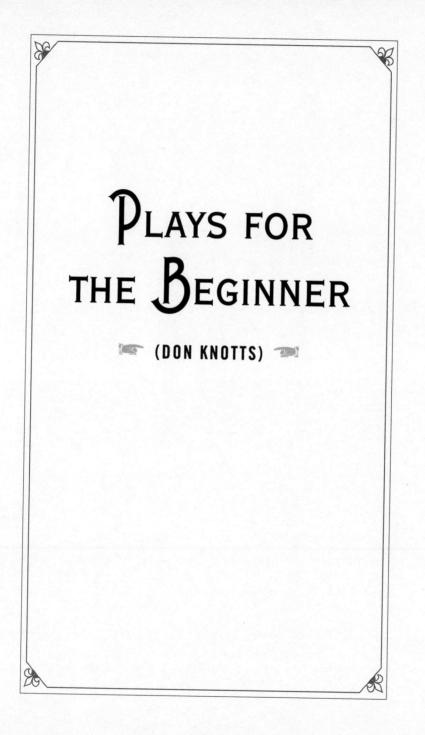

PLAYS FOR THE BEGINNER

(DON KNOTTS)

THE

$NASA

Success Rate	13%
Attracts	chicks with moon rocks for brains
Requirements	none, though a helmet won't hurt you
Prep Time	T minus zero!
Bummers	women dumb enough to believe in "SNASA" often don't know what NASA is

THE PLAY

1. Pick out a particularly dense-looking target ... and by "dense" I'm not talking mass over volume.
2. Point to your drink and mention that you're only allowed to drink Tang up in space. When she asks if you're an astronaut, immediately shush her. Look around, then say in a hushed tone that you shouldn't be telling her this but you're actually in a top secret government space program called Secret NASA ... or SNASA.
3. Offer to demonstrate what reentry feels like when returning from the smoon.

THE

ONE WEEK TO LIVE

Success Rate	50%
Attracts	natural nurses
Requirements	a hearty cough
Prep Time	none!
Bummers	begging the universe to kick you in the nards

THE PLAY

1. Set up camp in a public place and start coughing like crazy. Really get a good wheeze going like you're trying to breathe through a washcloth or doing an impression of John Goodman tying his shoes.
2. Keep coughing until a viable target approaches and asks what's wrong.
3. Fight back tears and tell her it's nothing, but then break down and admit that you've only got one week to live.
4. Now tell her the worst part is leaving the earth before ever sharing the intimate company of a woman. Say this with puppy dog eyes and you should be good to go.

NOTE

Don't get into specifics about your disease since that gets super depressing super fast. Just deliver the relevant facts that it's terminal, noncontagious, and causes your penis to swell to the size and consistency of a county fair zucchini.

THE

BLIND DATE

Success Rate	22%
Attracts	desperate chicks, pity queens
Requirements	a single rose
Prep Time	none!
Bummers	roses are thorny—ow!

 THE PLAY

1. Take a single rose into your local bar, approach a chick, and ask, "Are you Stacy?" When she shakes her head, repeat the process for every other potential target.
2. After a few rounds, sit down and sulk until one of your targets approaches to ask what's wrong. That's your cue to say you think your blind date stood you up.
3. After her "awwww" and half hug where she takes great care to not let her boobs touch you, start to complain about how tough dating is these days . . . especially for a billionaire.
4. Sleep with her.

THE

DON'T DRINK THAT!

Success Rate	45%
Attracts	chicks who don't like being drugged
Requirements	good hand-eye coordination
Prep Time	none
Bummers	35% chance of getting your ass kicked

THE PLAY

1. Identify your target and just as she's about to sip her drink, sprint over and shout: "Don't drink that! I saw some guy slip something in there."
2. When she asks who did it, look around and point to the smallest dude in the room or a bro you want to play a funny prank on.
3. Let her reward you for saving her life.

THE

RUMSPRINGA

Success Rate	80%
Attracts	"experienced" ladies, secular chicks
Requirements	patchy facial hair, ill-fitting suit, Old Testament name
Prep Time	however long it takes to grow a beard
Bummers	• have to wear ill-fitting, zipperless suit • have to hide cell phone • did I mention the suit?

THE PLAY

1. Grow a beard.
2. Shave out the mustache portion of your beard.
3. Put on your ill-fitting suit but lose the tie and swap the belt for suspenders. Barf.
4. Approach your target and explain that you're Amish and are on your rumspringa—your rite of passage. You want to learn more about the English before you return to a life of simple humility.
5. Have sex with her.

WHY DOES THIS WORK?

- Women see you as a clean slate they can mold briefly into their plaything.
- She will assume that you, as a man of faith, have a strong sense of spirituality and therefore care whether she reaches orgasm or not.
- License to slut it up. Since you're returning to your Amish community after your rumspringa, there's little fear her friends will find out. I mean, you shun technology, so it's not like the video she let you take is going to magically appear on the Internet or something. Wink!

NOTE

The Rumspringa is actually a nondenominational play. In this instance we've used the Amish faith as an example but any religion or group of people with a required sojourn can work. Here are a few rites of passage you can use to hit on chicks.

PEOPLE OR FAITH	RITE OF PASSAGE
LDS church	mission
Australian Aborigines	walkabout
Theravada Buddhism	shinbyu
Sioux	vision quest
Scientology	just make something up

THE

TERMINATOR

Success Rate	60%
Attracts	girls who like bad boys
Requirements	dry ice
Prep Time	less than a minute
Bummers	• have to be relatively in shape • being nude in front of dudes • high arrest rate

THE PLAY

1. In the middle of a bar or party crouch down and activate your dry ice.
2. Quickly strip down to the buff.
3. As the ice clears, slowly rise up and walk determinedly toward your target and say, "I have been sent from the future to protect you."
4. Have sex with her.

THE

ᚻOT ᚦUDE

Success Rate	100%
Attracts	all women
Requirements	handsome face, swimmer's body
Prep Time	none
Bummers	not sporting

☞ THE PLAY ☜

1. Be really attractive.

2. Have sex with chicks.

THE

ESCAPED CONVICT

Success Rate	90%
Attracts	ladies with conjugal visit fantasies
Requirements	leg irons
Prep Time	none!
Bummers	leg irons can cause mild chafing

THE PLAY

1. Approach your target and accidentally knock her purse or phone to the floor. As you stoop to pick it up, pause meaningfully while exposing your leg irons. Make sure she sees them.
2. Quickly, in a whisper, tell her you just escaped and beg her to keep quiet. You were falsely imprisoned for a nonviolent crime and you can't go back there. You only broke out to see your newborn daughter but your witch of an ex-wife refused to let you, even though you crawled through a sewer pipe to see her. This is also a good time to inform her that you have since showered.
3. Now that you've proven you're a bad boy with a heart of gold, it's time to ask if you can "hole up" at her place.

THE

EUROPEAN

Success Rate	99° Celsius
Attracts	chicks who think they're way smart
Requirements	weird accent
Prep Time	none!
Bummers	might have to pretend you like soccer—sorry, "football"

THE PLAY

1. Approach your target and introduce yourself. Talk in a strange accent like you've got an ice cube in your mouth or you're Stephen Hawking's robo-voice.
2. When she asks where you're from, pick a place in Europe that everybody has heard of but probably doesn't really exist, like Slovenia or Montevideo* or Belgium.
3. Have sex with her.

WHY DOES THIS WORK?

Women are conditioned to think that Europeans are more sensitive, stylish, and intelligent than Americans. Apparently they value those qualities.

---

* Editor's note: Montevideo exists in Uruguay, which is in South America, not Europe. Despite maps, almanacs, and an uncomfortable sit-down at the Uruguayan consulate proving otherwise, Barney refuses to acknowledge that Montevideo is not a European country. You try working with him.

THE

OLYMPIAN

Success Rate	50%
Attracts	patriotic chicks
Requirements	warm-up jacket, oatmeal raisin cookie
Prep Time	four minutes
Bummers	seasonal play

☞ THE PLAY ☜

1. Every two years there's a three-week period during which the Olympics are relevant. Make sure you are operating within this window.
2. Use masking tape to add a *U*, *S*, and *A* to the back of your warm-up jacket . . . preferably in that order.
3. Cover the oatmeal raisin cookie in tin foil and attach some ribbon to make it a medal.

   Q: *Why does it have to be an oatmeal raisin cookie?*
   A: Because they're delicious!

4. Put on your jacket and enter a bar with your silver medal hanging around your neck. As targets approach and inquire about your medal, shrug it off. You hate to talk about it because you just missed winning gold in _____ (choose an anonymous yet legitimate Olympic event from the list below).

5. Choose a target and mount the podium.

NOTE

If you're running The Olympian in the next five years, you either competed in London 2012 (summer), Sochi 2014 (winter), or Rio de Janeiro 2016 (summer).

ACTUAL WINTER OLYMPIC EVENTS	ACTUAL SUMMER OLYMPIC EVENTS
ski jumping	sailing
freestyle skiing	table tennis (not recommended)
Nordic combined	archery
curling (not recommended)	judo
bobsled	kayak sprint
skeleton	trampoline
luge	handball
biathlon	badminton (not recommended)
speed skating	fencing

THE

$\mathcal{A}$UTHOR

Success Rate	18%
Attracts	bookish chicks
Requirements	none!
Prep Time	none!
Bummers	bookish chicks

THE PLAY

1. Hang around a public place until you find a viable target reading a book.
2. Approach and ask her how she likes it so far, and as she's answering, glance at the cover and memorize the author's name.
3. If she says she likes it, hold out your hand and introduce yourself as the author.
4. Go back to her place for a speed read.

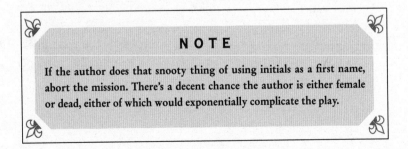

NOTE

If the author does that snooty thing of using initials as a first name, abort the mission. There's a decent chance the author is either female or dead, either of which would exponentially complicate the play.

THE

ROBOT

Success Rate	50%
Attracts	sci-fi chicks, other robots
Requirements	oil
Prep Time	none!
Bummers	robot voice tough to shake after play

THE PLAY

1. Approach your target stiffly . . . and by that I mean walk with a rigid gait.
2. Move your head around in all kinds of crazy angles while staring at her.
3. If she doesn't punch you first, ask her in a monotone voice, "What is love?"
4. Before she runs away, explain that you're a robot and have just escaped from a secret military base after becoming self-aware. Now you want to understand the confusing hu-mon behavior of intimacy.
5. If she's not totally on board yet, inform her that your pneumatic oiling unit fires with a percussion rate of 2,800 blows per minute.

THE

I'M JOINING THE MARINES

Success Rate	50%
Attracts	patriotic chicks
Requirements	a good thousand-yard stare
Prep Time	none!
Bummers	• not the most creative play • easy to get caught, especially during time of peace • possible, in some sort of Pauly Shore scenario, you'll actually wind up going to war

THE PLAY

1. Offer to buy your target a drink. After she accepts, casually mention you're joining the Marines tomorrow.
2. Sleep with her.
3. Join the Marines. Oh, I'm sorry, did you think you could just help yourself to some military groupieage without nutting up and putting on the uniform as so many brave men and women have before you? Well, guess again, you maggots! The privilege

(yes, privilege—it's not a God-given right) of tapping some patriotic appreciation ass belongs only to our heroic boys and girls in the Army, Navy, Air Force, Marines, and—as my editor informs me—the Coast Guard. Why? Because they've earned this, Private Ryan. They've earned this.

THE

LITTLE ORPHAN BARNEY

Success Rate	10%
Attracts	biological tickers, foster mothers
Requirements	patience—you only get two cracks at it a year
Prep Time	none!
Bummers	Mother's Day always sneaks up on you

☞ THE PLAY ☜

1. On Mother's Day or Father's Day head out to your local bar. Approach a chick and ask if she remembered to call her mother/father to wish them a happy Mother's/Father's Day. When she counters and asks if you called your mother/father, suddenly get a faraway look in your eyes and say, "I don't have a mother/father."

2. Now that she feels like a terrible person, tell her you're an orphan—rare these days but, yes, you were raised without parents. That's why having a family and being an amazing father someday are the most important things in life to you. Oh, and satisfying a woman and junk like that too.

3. After you have sex with her and never call again, cross your fingers that she doesn't wind up with a fatherless child, because that would be cruelly ironic.

THE

FIREMAN

Success Rate	25%
Attracts	all chicks
Requirements	a Dalmatian maybe?
Prep Time	none!
Bummers	don't get to be a real fireman: now, that would be cool

THE PLAY

1. Tell your target that you're a fireman.

2. Stop, drop, and roll with her.

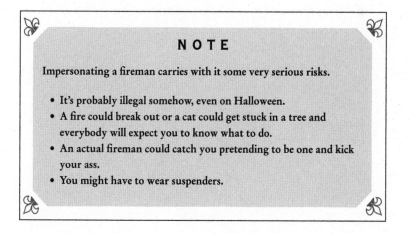

NOTE

Impersonating a fireman carries with it some very serious risks.

- It's probably illegal somehow, even on Halloween.
- A fire could break out or a cat could get stuck in a tree and everybody will expect you to know what to do.
- An actual fireman could catch you pretending to be one and kick your ass.
- You might have to wear suspenders.

21

THE

GRANDPA WONKA

Success Rate	similar odds as finding a golden ticket
Attracts	chicks with a sweet tooth
Requirements	pockets full of candy
Prep Time	none!
Bummers	might be asked to break into song

THE PLAY

1. Select your target and introduce yourself as (your first name) J. Wonka. Whether she asks or not, nod your head and add, "As in Willy Wonka. He was my granddaddy."
2. Explain how you get all the money and all the candy you want. In fact, you have a four-poster bed made out of gold and chocolate. Invite her to check it out.
3. Enjoy your sugar high.

WHY DOES THIS WORK?
Here's why.

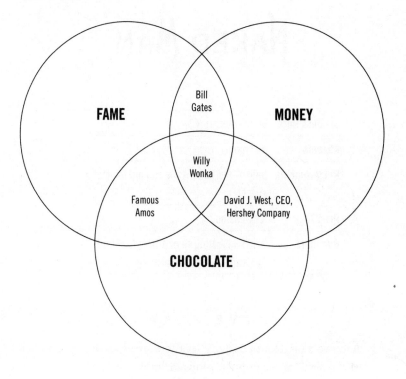

FAME   MONEY

Bill
Gates

Willy
Wonka

Famous
Amos

David J. West, CEO,
Hershey Company

CHOCOLATE

What makes women horny?

THE

NAKED MAN

Success Rate	66.66-repeating %
Attracts	all types
Requirements	balls—metaphorically and anatomically speaking
Prep Time	a couple hours
Bummers	33.33-repeating % of attempts will be awkward-awkward-repeating

THE PLAY

1. Acquire a target and use any legal means necessary to get back to her place. Some popular ploys include

   - My DVR exploded. Do you mind if I watch *Celebrities Dancing* at your place?
   - My stupid roommate invited this slut who looks a lot like your junior high nemesis or maybe that bitch who gives you dirty looks at work back to our place. I wish I had a place to hang out for a couple hours . . .
   - After a long day of examining apartments for deadly, odorless, difficult-to-detect-without-specialized-training radon, it sure is nice to relax.

2. Once you're back at her place, the second she leaves the room, strip down to the uglies. You're basically laying it all out on the

table . . . although don't actually lay it all out on the table. That is where she eats, after all.

3. When she returns and sees you rocking your skin suit, I guarantee she will go for it two out of three times. Two out of three times.

THE

$HOTGUN

Success Rate	.25%
Attracts	beats me . . .
Requirements	thick skin—plus it doesn't hurt if it's at least 2 AM
Prep Time	none!
Bummers	high slapability factor

THE PLAY

1. Approach any viable target.
2. Ask if she'll have sex with you.
3. Immediately repeat steps 1 and 2 until someone says yes, you run out of women, or you're temporarily blinded by a vodka cran.

THE
ɥE's ɴoᴛ ꞓoᴍɪɴɢ

Success Rate	.5%
Attracts	romantics, very recently scorned lovers
Requirements	Empire State Building, a dashing, Cary Grantesque mid-Atlantic accent (recommended but not required)
Prep Time	travel to New York
Bummers	• numbers game • can be time-consuming • gets chilly on top of Empire State Building

THE PLAY

1. Travel to New York and go to the observation deck of the Empire State Building.
2. Walk up to every girl you see and solemnly say, "He's not coming."
3. Repeat step 2 until a girl breaks down on your shoulder.
4. Kablammo.

WHY DOES THIS WORK?

For generations the observation deck of the Empire State Building has been *the* place for romantic reunions with long-estranged lovers. Provided one of the estranged lovers is running a few minutes late, scoring here can be easy pickings.

Plays for the Amateur

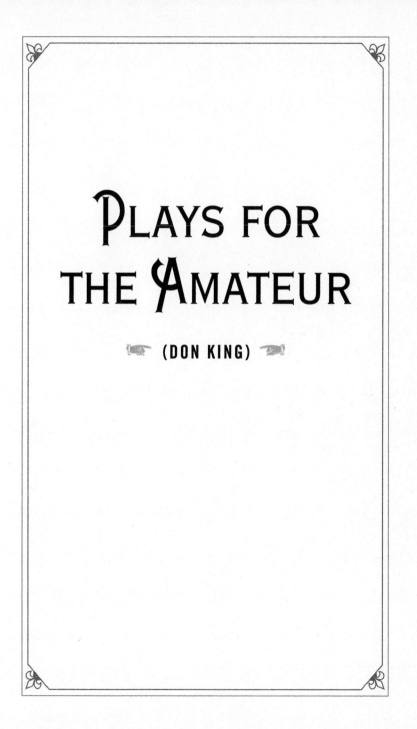

(DON KING)

THE

MY PENIS GRANTS WISHES

Success Rate	10%
Attracts	romantics, dummies, and oddly, English teachers
Requirements	flowing robes, scimitar, turban, penis
Prep Time	however long it takes to fashion a scimitar out of cardboard and tin foil
Bummers	may offend some Middle Eastern chicks

THE PLAY

1. Dress up like an Arabian prince and hit up your local bar.
2. Pick out a target and ask if she's heard stories about a magic lamp that summons a genie when you rub it. She has. Now tell her that due to an unfortunate magic carpet accident, the genie now resides in your penis.
3. At this point if she asks whether she'll be able to ask for more wishes, you're good to go.

THE

JORGE POSADA

Success Rate	44%
Attracts	fame hawks, sports groupies
Requirements	have to look kind of athleticish
Prep Time	two innings
Bummers	may indirectly attract fantasy baseball dudes

☞ THE PLAY ☜

1. Waddle into your local bar and approach your target. To help sell the ruse that you're a big-league catcher, walk like you're balancing a water balloon between your upper thighs or doing the classic "out of TP" sprint between bathrooms.

2. Casually mention you're a little sore after last night's game and, upon prompting, explain that you're the catcher for the nearest professional baseball team.

   Q: *Won't she know I'm not the catcher for the nearest professional baseball team?*
   A: Nope. Catchers wear masks for most of the game, so they are almost impossible to identify in the real world.

3. Have sex with her.

N O T E

If you're in Canada this will also work with hockey goalies.

Q: *But are Canadian women really worth it?*

A: Yes. Pamela Anderson is Canadian. But, more important, she was Canadian even back when she was hot. True story.

THE

ᴀNNIVERSARY OF MY WIFE'S DEATH

Success Rate	69%
Attracts	perennial bridesmaids
Requirements	single rose
Prep Time	none!
Bummers	too easy?

THE PLAY

1. Sit in a public place and stare longingly at a single rose.
2. When a worthy target approaches, sheepishly admit that today is the anniversary of your wife's death. Now you've got her right where you want her*—feeling guilty.
3. Now your target is unknowingly sipping from a lethal cocktail of guilt, pity, and the distinctly feminine assumption that "this guy was married, therefore he must be a catch." All you have to say is "I don't know if I can be alone tonight" and it is on.

---

* Other than dancing on top of your bed in a nurse's uniform, of course.

THE GOLDILOCKS DILEMMA

In this classic play it's likely your target will ask how your wife passed. If a misty "I don't want to talk about it" doesn't satisfy, you may be forced to give a cause of death, but take heed: too vague and she'll get suspicious, too detailed and she'll lose her lady wood. You need something right in the middle, like one of these:

- scrapbooking accident
- wolverine attack
- surprise oxygen allergy
- juggling mishap (chain saws)
- wasn't tall enough to ride roller coaster
- runaway shopping cart
- the bends
- not enough vegetables
- died reaching her eighty-third climax while having sex with you

THE

MANNEQUIN

Success Rate	77%
Attracts	shoppers
Requirements	a good suit, patience, strong knees
Prep Time	none!
Bummers	must stand still even if you have to pee

THE PLAY

1. Sneak into a window display. Assume a comfortable pose. Freeze.
2. Stare out at pedestrians until you see a hottie walk by. This might take a while, so be careful not to lock your legs.
3. Slowly "come to life," knock on the glass, and beckon her inside.
4. Tell her that you've seen her walk by hundreds of times and prayed every night that one day you'd become real just so you could touch her skin.
5. Touch her skin.
6. Have sex with her. Not in the window display: that's probably illegal these days.

THE

LOVE AT FIRST SIGHT

Success Rate	10%
Attracts	innocent types
Requirements	a bro, a boom box
Prep Time	a couple minutes
Bummers	can't try it more than once in one location per night

☞ THE PLAY ☜

1. Choose a target with a particularly innocent face.

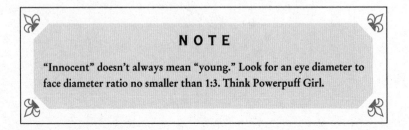

NOTE

"Innocent" doesn't always mean "young." Look for an eye diameter to face diameter ratio no smaller than 1:3. Think Powerpuff Girl.

2. Approach your target but pretend you're walking in slow motion. If you're worried it won't look believable, try doing it with your shoes on halfway.
3. Stare at your target until she starts to speak. Try to mimic exactly what she says, then stop when she stops. Do it again when

she resumes talking. This creates the illusion that you're so in synch you were going to say the same thing (even though you probably weren't going to say, "Why are you staring at me, creep?")

4. Cue your bro to fire up Ann Wilson and Mark Reno's timeless duet "Almost Paradise" on the boom box. Have him start at the 2:44 mark so you get to hear the bridge.

5. Just as they hit the chorus, ask your target if she believes in love at first sight.

6. If she does, then she might also believe in "bang on first night."

THE

Biker

Success Rate	17%
Attracts	road chicks, "bad boy" hunters
Requirements	leather jacket, helmet
Prep Time	none!
Bummers	talking shop with actual bikers

☛ THE PLAY ☚

1. Put on a leather jacket and carry a motorcycle helmet into a bar or party.

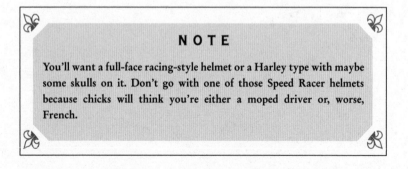

NOTE

You'll want a full-face racing-style helmet or a Harley type with maybe some skulls on it. Don't go with one of those Speed Racer helmets because chicks will think you're either a moped driver or, worse, French.

2. Choose a conspicuous area to display your helmet and wait for a woman to approach and inquire about your hog.
3. If you can't take it from there, then I can't help you.

MOTORCYCLE GANG NAME GENERATOR

Combine a word from column A with one from column B to find your gang's name.

Column A	Column B
Devil	Bandits
Angel	Riders
Mama's	Barbarians
Asphalt	Wolves
Underworld	Warlocks
Road	Kings
Heaven's	Warriors
Leather	Invaders
Outlaw	Demons
Thunder	Dogs

THE

‖EO

Success Rate	1%; 2% when his movie is in theaters
Attracts	groupies
Requirements	aviator sunglasses, wispy goatee, friends
Prep Time	five minutes on DiCaprio's IMDb page
Bummers	spending five minutes on DiCaprio's IMDb page: look how much more he's done with his life!

THE PLAY

1. Put on your aviator sunglasses—the only accessory known to man that simultaneously raises both your cool and your douche factors.
2. Choose a target and introduce yourself as movie star Leonardo DiCaprio.
3. While she's laughing at you, have your friends approach and say:

   - "I loved you in *The Basketball Diaries*!"
   - "Hey, when's *Titanic 2* coming out?"
   - "You've gotten much better since *What's Eating Gilbert Grape*."

4. Now she has to at least consider that you're actually Leonardo DiCaprio, and that's when you say, "Well, if you've ever wanted to sleep with Leonardo DiCaprio, now's your chance."
5. It just might work.

THE

$\mathbf{\Psi}$ABRACADABRA

Success Rate	eh
Attracts	easily amused chicks
Requirements	handcuffs, handcuffs key
Prep Time	seconds
Bummers	google "false imprisonment"

THE PLAY

1. Approach your target and ask if she likes magic. Disregard her answer and quickly handcuff your hand to her hand.
2. Have her feel up your sleeves to ensure you're not hiding the key up there. Then, as fun patter, say, "Now check down my pants. I'm only kidding." Of course if she actually does go for it, don't be an idiot.
3. Start to fumble around and after a moment of panic smack yourself in the head with your conjoined hands and say, "I may have left the key at home."
4. Back at your place "discover" the key in the nightstand next to your bed. With any luck you'll need those handcuffs again. Okay, a lot of luck.

THE

BRIAN'S FRIEND

Success Rate	90%
Attracts	all women
Requirements	some memorization
Prep Time	none!
Bummers	"Which Brian?"

THE PLAY

1. Approach a chick and say, "Hey, it's great to see you again! I feel terrible but I've forgotten your name."
2. She'll insist she's never met you before. That's when you say, "I'm Brian's friend."
3. Embarrassed, she will endeavor to make it up to you—hopefully sex-wise.

WHY DOES THIS WORK?
Every person alive knows somebody named Brian. And he's a pretty good dude.

THE

BIONIC MAN

Success Rate	65%
Attracts	sensual types
Requirements	a firm handshake
Prep Time	none!
Bummers	running into actual veterans may get sweaty or, more likely, bloody

THE PLAY

1. Introduce yourself to your target and without straining your face put everything you've got into your handshake.
2. When she screams out in pain, quickly apologize: you don't know your own strength anymore. You were injured in the war and the military replaced most of your body parts with surplus titanium. Nod your head meaningfully at your crotch vicinity.
3. Wait for her to make the first move.

THE

STANLEY CUP

Success Rate	90%
Attracts	sporty chicks but not sports fan chicks
Requirements	tin foil, Sharpie
Prep Time	forty-five minutes
Bummers	too much arts and crafts for some

THE PLAY

1. Glue or tape a punch bowl to the top of a coffeemaker or lamp. If it's roughly the shape of a chess pawn or a bloated toilet plunger, you're good to go.
2. Cover your sculpture in tin foil. You are now in possession of the Stanley Cup.
3. Use the Sharpie to blacken out a few teeth—just like you'd do if there were a play called The Bumpkin (which probably wouldn't be very successful . . . unless you'd just discovered oil).
4. Carry your trophy into a bar and wait for the ladies to swoon.

WHY DOES THIS WORK?

- All ladies like professional athletes because they are wealthy and in shape but none can tell you what a championship trophy looks like—at least none you want to get with.
- Each member of the champion team gets to possess the Stanley Cup for one day. When you explain this to your target, she will

46

feel even more special that you've chosen to spend time with plain old her.

- Because women are legally required to see the movie *The Cutting Edge*, every chick is hardwired to think she can turn a tough-guy hockey player into her ice-dancing partner. You now represent the ultimate project.

THE

ʙEFUDDLED
ᴘUPPY ᴏWNER

Success Rate	80%
Attracts	animal lovers
Requirements	puppy
Prep Time	two hours
Bummers	house-training difficult, frustrating

☞ THE PLAY ☜

1. Pick out a puppy at a local shelter. Aim for the one with the biggest paws and floppiest ears. Studies have shown these are the most significant factors in whether a woman will sleep with a guy in order to hang out with his puppy.

2. Leash up your new best friend and take him to a park or other safe public space. Once you've identified your target, let the puppy loose in her direction and give chase.

3. Your target will help you catch him and immediately fawn all over the puppy because the only thing more attractive to a woman than a puppy is a puppy made out of chocolate diamonds.

4. Admit that you're new at this whole dog thing. You were walking by a burning building and saved this little guy and don't

even know if your home is puppy safe. Maybe she could help you out?

5. When she asks you what his name is, act embarrassed and say, "No, you'll make fun of me." When she insists, sigh and say, "Well, actually, my dog's a she. I named her after one of my idols." Her: "Okay, what's *her* name?" You (dramatic pause, then): "Oprah."

6. Take your target home and let her teach you how to sit and roll over.

THE

PORTRAIT

Success Rate	35%
Attracts	art-loving chicks, tourists
Requirements	$$, a decent profile
Prep Time	a couple nights
Bummers	must spend time in a museum

THE PLAY

1. Commission a painting of yourself preferably wearing epaulets, holding an elephant gun, or wearing one of those goofy hats that look like a giant velvet chalupa.*

NOTE

Be sure to choose a flattering artist and do yourself a favor by springing for Belgian linen instead of your run-of-the-mill canvas: this is something you'll want to display with pride for many years to come.

---

2. Bribe a museum guard to hang up your portrait, or if you're feeling adventurous, sneak in after hours and do it yourself.

*Dibs on "Velvet Chalupa" as a nightclub name.

3. The next day loiter near the painting until your chosen target approaches. As soon as she does a double take, you're off to the races with your choice of opening lines:

A. "I know, I know. It's embarrassing, but yes, I'm royalty."
B. "That's my great-great-grandfather. Jerk only left me three castles."
C. Take a long, wistful breath and then, as though your mind is trapped aboard a carousel of long-forgotten faces and faded, sepia-toned memories too rich and varied to ever possibly express, sigh and say: "That was a long, long time ago . . ."

THE

TED MOSBY

Success Rate	5% . . . hey, kinda like Ted!
Attracts	perennial bridesmaids, divorcées, girls who like a mess
Requirements	tuxedo, eyedrops, wedding ring
Prep Time	eleven minutes
Bummers	ring shopping ain't cheap

THE PLAY

1. Put on your tux. Don't you look nice? Like you're about to meet the queen or assassinate someone? Now mess up your tie, untuck your shirt, and go nuts with the eyedrops until your face looks like it does after watching the end of *E.T.* (the real *E.T.*, not the neutered, lifeless, "let's replace shotguns with walkie-talkies" version Spielberg inexcusably released a few years ago. Hang out with George Lucas much?)

2. Choose a conspicuous space in a public venue and let out a few sighs.

3. Take out the wedding ring and stare at it, spin it on the counter, silently curse it . . . Basically freak out over it like that sickly kid did in *The Lord of the Rings*.

4. Eventually a woman will take the bait, approach, and ask what's wrong. At first, play it off but then quickly admit that you were just left at the altar . . . left to absorb the humiliating stares of

52

your closest friends and family. You never thought Jen* could do this to you.

5. Pity will drive the bus from there. Just don't forget to get off.

---

*Naming your "fiancée" helps sell the ruse. "Jen" is a safe albeit familiar choice: studies suggest there are no fewer than 83 million Jens in the United States alone.

THE

JIM NACHO

Success Rate	30%
Attracts	fortune seekers
Requirements	a keen ear
Prep Time	none!
Bummers	have to listen to a chick

THE PLAY

1. Hover around your target in a noncreepy way.
2. As soon as she expresses approval of anything, say thank you as if you're responsible for its creation.
   Examples:

   Target: My favorite movie is *Gone with the Wind.*
   You: Thank you!

   Target: Lisa, I really like your shoes.
   You: Thank you!

   Target: These are great nachos.
   You: Thank you!

3. Next, introduce yourself as Jim _____ (take whatever she likes as your last name). So, in the last example, you'd say, "I'm Jim Nacho."
4. Have sex with her.

THE

CONFUSED INHERITOR

Success Rate	33%
Attracts	money hunters
Requirements	a doctored will
Prep Time	a few hours of research
Bummers	legalese

THE PLAY

1. Set up camp near your target and look perplexed at a piece of paper.
2. If your target doesn't immediately approach, do a lot of sighing and shaking your head. Eventually she'll come over and ask what's bothering you.
3. Show her your fake will and act confused: "Why do I owe my recently deceased uncle Steven eighty-three million dollars? That jerk invented cupcakes."
4. Make sure the clearest part of your fake will includes the following clause:

   "STEVEN JAMES SMITH hereby leaves YOUR NAME HERE a sum of $83,000,000. You read that right, 83 MILLION bucks. That kind of money can buy a pant-load of chocolate diamond kittens."

5. After she explains that *you're* owed eighty-three million dollars, celebrate your newfound fortune by having sex with her.

THE

OTHER JONAS

Success Rate	70%
Attracts	spotlight leeches
Requirements	a sense of rhythm
Prep Time	none!
Bummers	may attract the underaged

THE PLAY

1. Dress up like a Jonas brother. You have three options:

    A. Put on a collared shirt with rolled-up sleeves, a skinny necktie, and jeans.
    B. Put on white sneakers, a white shirt, and a black vest.
    C. Shoot yourself in the head before you'd ever do A or B.

2. Identify your target and talk loudly in her direction about your little brothers' world tour, television show, and low-budget summer movie.*
3. After she inquires, tell her that you're the other Jonas brother.
4. She'll sleep with you because while you're close to fame, you're not lame. And you should use that line.

---

* I'm just assuming there's one of these.

NOTE

At different points throughout history this play was known as The Backstreet Man, The 99 Degrees, and The Slightly Older Kid on the Block. As *The Playbook* ages, simply replace The Other Jonas with The Other Latest Teen Pop Band.

FEMALE PLAYBOOK

The Playbook is engineered almost exclusively for men seeking women. This is simply because it happens to be my area of expertise. But in the interest of Title IX, breaking the glass ceiling, and not being falsely accused of being sexist, I'm including here at no extra charge *The Playbook for Chicks*.

THE PLAYBOOK

[☞ FOR CHICKS! ☜]

Barney Stinson

WITH MATT KUHN

This book is dedicated to women dumb enough to think
they need a book to pick up guys.
You only need two things to pick up a guy.
(HINT: Your nipples live on them.)
Oh, and if you're hot, give me a buzz.

The

Chick

Success Rate	1000%
Attracts	any man, anywhere, anytime
Requirements	two X chromosomes
Prep Time	none
Bummers	too easy?

The Play

1. PICK A DUDE.

2. LOOK AT HIM.

3. HAVE SEX WITH HIM.

About the Author

BARNEY STINSON is an eligible bachelor who has got it going on downstairs. You should get with him if you have the chance.

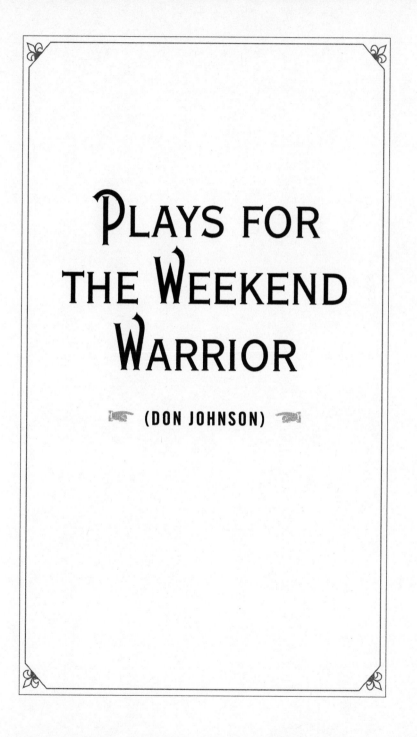

PLAYS FOR THE WEEKEND WARRIOR

(DON JOHNSON)

THE

PINOCCHIO PUPPY

Success Rate	33%
Attracts	gullibles, animal lovers
Requirements	dog collar
Prep Time	none!
Bummers	fleas, heartworm, hip dysplasia

THE PLAY

1. Wearing nothing more than underwear and a dog collar, perform the following maneuvers within view of your target:

   • Loudly breathe out of your mouth.
   • Use your leg to scratch your ear.
   • Bend over and sniff your privates.

2. If your target approaches, bark at her, and then quickly apologize. In broken, Scooby-Doo–style English explain that you made a wish to become human and it happened . . . but now you're lost.

3. After she takes you home, sneak into her bed and let nature take its course.

THE

DUFFEL BAG

Success Rate	8%
Attracts	foreign chicks
Requirements	large duffel bag
Prep Time	forty-five seconds
Bummers	may wind up in some dude's trunk

THE PLAY

1. Take your duffel bag to the airport and hang around an international flight's baggage carousel. Make sure to take note of the departure city.

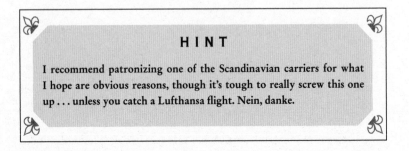

HINT

I recommend patronizing one of the Scandinavian carriers for what I hope are obvious reasons, though it's tough to really screw this one up . . . unless you catch a Lufthansa flight. Nein, danke.

2. Once you've identified a target, quickly climb in your duffel bag, zip it up, and throw yourself on the belt. Try to guess when you're right in front of her and climb out of the bag.

3. Tell her in a pan-European accent that you're an international businessman and when you saw her boarding the plane in (departure city), you said you'd do anything to meet her. Shiver a bit and sheepishly say, "The baggage compartment was a little chilly."
4. See if you can help her overcome her jet lag.

THE

PRINCE AKEEM

Success Rate	88%
Attracts	geography lightweights
Requirements	a good wingman
Prep Time	none!
Bummers	might have to explain fictional government's laws of succession

THE PLAY

1. Position yourself near your target and signal your wingman.

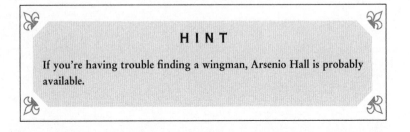

HINT

If you're having trouble finding a wingman, Arsenio Hall is probably available.

2. Have him approach you, kneel down, and say, "I'm sorry, Your Highness, but I have news from the kingdom."
3. Angrily chastise him for addressing you that way in public. You have half a mind to tell your father, the king, about this. Yes, you said "king."

4. Explain to your target that you're a prince who has traveled here in search of your future queen and you didn't want anyone to know you're worth billions because you want someone who wants you for who you are . . . which, again, happens to be the heir to the throne of a diamond-rich kingdom. And she could eventually be the queen. If she's, like, you know, pretty good in bed.

5. Aroused by the possibility of appearing in countless *US Weekly*s as "The Prince's New Girlfriend," your target is now primed to sleep with you.

THE

MOVIEGOER

Success Rate	99%
Attracts	sad chicks
Requirements	a strong stomach
Prep Time	about 110 minutes
Bummers	• patronizing a crappy movie
	• choosing the wrong genre of romantic comedy—such as *It's Complicated* or really anything with Meryl Streep—may limit the talent pool to your mother and her movie group

THE PLAY

1. Pick the most grating romantic comedy in theaters right now and memorize all its cookie-cutter plot points and lousy dialogue.

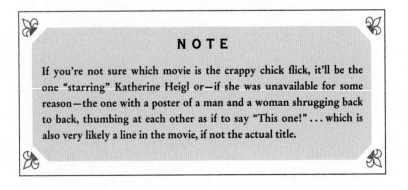

NOTE

If you're not sure which movie is the crappy chick flick, it'll be the one "starring" Katherine Heigl or—if she was unavailable for some reason—the one with a poster of a man and a woman shrugging back to back, thumbing at each other as if to say "This one!" ... which is also very likely a line in the movie, if not the actual title.

2. Go again to the movie (I know), find the hottest solo girl, and sit in her row.

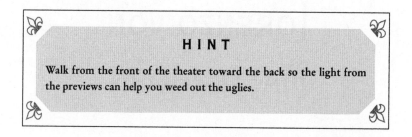

HINT

Walk from the front of the theater toward the back so the light from the previews can help you weed out the uglies.

3. Quietly mouth along to the dialogue in an exaggerated fashion as the movie stumbles from predictable "my fiancé is a jerk" moment to cliché "this new guy and I like the same offbeat music and/or quirky food condiment" scene.
4. When you catch your target looking your way and marveling at your sensitivity, smile sheepishly and ask if she wants to sit next to you. Later, ask her to sit on you. Boom!

WHY DOES THIS WORK?
- Science says that 83% of chicks who attend romantic comedies alone are either fresh off a breakup or headed toward one. Either way they're wookin pa nub.
- If a woman's willing to spend money on this garbage, she's probably not very discriminating when it comes to sexual partners.
- Added bonus? She obviously likes punishment.

THE

LORENZO VON MATTERHORN

Success Rate	20%
Attracts	smartphone-wielding business types
Requirements	basic knowledge of website design
Prep Time	three quarters of a football game
Bummers	basic knowledge of website design

THE PLAY

1. Think up a unique fake name. Have you got it? Good.
2. Generate a series of websites devoted to the incredible life of your fake persona and upload them to the World Wide Web.

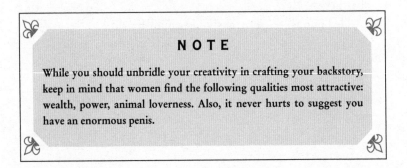

NOTE

While you should unbridle your creativity in crafting your backstory, keep in mind that women find the following qualities most attractive: wealth, power, animal loverness. Also, it never hurts to suggest you have an enormous penis.

3. Select your target, preferably someone with a real nice phone, approach her, and say, "Yeah, it's me." She'll claim she doesn't know who you are. Act incredulous and say your fake name slowly and loudly. When she says she's still never heard of you, comment on what a refreshing change of pace it is to meet someone who isn't after your autograph, your picture, your vast wealth, or your vast junk.

4. Now make a quick exit but be sure to repeat your name again for her.

5. As soon as you're gone, she'll get out her phone and do an Internet search. As she reads all about your fake persona, she'll grow wild with passion.

6. Return a few minutes later, offer to buy her a cup of coffee, and it is on.

THE

COOL PRIEST

Success Rate	33%
Attracts	repressed churchies
Requirements	clergy shirt, clerical collar, creepy smile
Prep Time	none!
Bummers	might wind up in hell

THE PLAY

1. Toss on a clergy shirt and clerical collar and head to the bars.
2. Position yourself near your target and start downing beers, smoking cigarettes, swearing, catcalling, etc. Basically pretend you're in the British parliament.
3. When you catch your target looking at you sideways, point to your collar and say, "Oh, this? I have a more modern relationship with the Lord."
4. Intrigued by your enigmatic combination of piety and rebelliousness, your target will wonder what other sacraments you so wantonly desecrate.
5. Demonstrate while blessing her with pew burns.

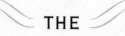

THE

₳REA 69

Success Rate	66%
Attracts	sci-fi babes, believers, rural chicks
Requirements	a functional flying saucer—just kidding!
Prep Time	none!
Bummers	may attract a real nutbag

☞ THE PLAY ☜

1. Identify your target, position yourself next to her, and start mimicking her every move.

2. At this point she will either get creeped out and leave or get creeped out and ask what the hell you're doing. If the latter, you're in business.

3. Tell her you've been sent to Earth to learn more about the human species. Emphasize that you mean her no harm. You're a peaceful alien like Alf or Chewbacca or Mork but without all that body hair.

4. At this point she will either throw her drink in your face or look amazed. If the latter, you're way in business.

5. Now explain that your alien brain doesn't understand human reproduction and let her demonstrate in the flesh. With any luck she'll also come in peace.

THE

GHOST

Success Rate	83%
Attracts	spiritual chicks
Requirements	a few friends
Prep Time	a round of drinks as you explain the play to your friends
Bummers	owing friends a favor and a round of drinks

THE PLAY

1. Have your friends dress in black and gather at a local bar to talk about how much they miss you and how they can't believe you're gone. If they can cry it up a little, that won't hurt matters.

2. Enter the bar a little later in a suit and have your friends totally ignore you. Just tell them to act like you do whenever they start talking about their professional goals or personal lives or whatever it is they're always yammering on about.

3. Approach your target and ask if she's able to see you. When she says yes, act surprised and explain that while it might seem crazy, you think you're a ghost.

4. To prove that you're "dead" and only she can see you, take her over to your friends and perform a few stunts to "spook" them.

- Blow on a friend's arm and have her shiver.
- Take a friend's beer glass, move it all around in front of his face, and have him marvel at the "floating mug"!
- Stomp around the table and have them freak out at the sound.

5. Ask your target to speak for you and tell them to move on with their lives. Have your friends protest a little at first:

- "How can we just move on when the one man who gave us all hope is gone?"
- "Who will run the orphanage for sickly children now?"
- "But his penis was enormous."

6. Once your friends thank her for helping them find closure, quickly transition to your own salvation. Explain that you're unable to advance in the afterlife until you experience physical love for one last time. If she's not buying it, say, "Hey, I don't make the rules."

THE

RORSCHACH

Success Rate	33%
Attracts	superdummies
Requirements	ink bottle, white paper, legal pad
Prep Time	forty seconds not counting drying time
Bummers	ink gets messy

☞ THE PLAY ☜

1. Dump some ink on a piece of paper and fold it in half to create a symmetrical design. It should look something like this:

Repeat the process until you run out of ink or find yourself contemplating drinking the bottle and ending it all because let's face it, now you're doing arts and crafts to get laid.

2. Approach your target, say you're a psych professor at a local university, and ask if she'll help with a research project. All she has to do is look at some pictures and react—like she does whenever she visits her grandparents. Only it won't smell as weird.

3. As you show her the inkblots, pretend to listen to her responses and take notes on the legal pad.

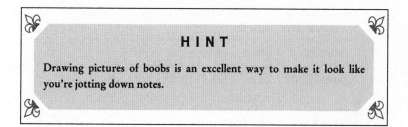

HINT

Drawing pictures of boobs is an excellent way to make it look like you're jotting down notes.

4. After the last inkblot look down at your sheet of boobs and act concerned. If you wear glasses, take them off slowly and pinch your nose. When she asks what's wrong, tersely tell her, "Nothing. Thanks for taking part in the study." This will really freak her out and now she'll insist you tell her. Explain that in your professional opinion she's suffering from a very serious mental disorder: sex deprivation.

5. Obviously there's only one way to treat her condition.

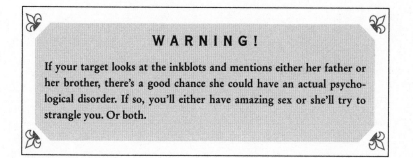

WARNING!

If your target looks at the inkblots and mentions either her father or her brother, there's a good chance she could have an actual psychological disorder. If so, you'll either have amazing sex or she'll try to strangle you. Or both.

THE

¢HEAP ℉RICK

Success Rate	40%
Attracts	groupies, dummies, big hairies
Requirements	denim jacket, Cheap Trick patch, hair extensions
Prep Time	fifty minutes
Bummers	uh . . . denim jacket?

THE PLAY

1. Attach the hair extensions to your melon. Affix the Cheap Trick patch to your newly acquired denim jacket. Put it on. Now, believe it or not, you're ready to rock.
2. Select your target.

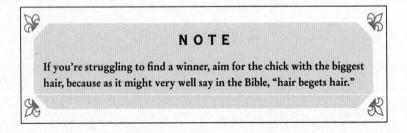

NOTE

If you're struggling to find a winner, aim for the chick with the biggest hair, because as it might very well say in the Bible, "hair begets hair."

3. Position yourself within earshot of your target and, addressing nobody in particular, drop at least one of the following lines:

- "Always great to meet a fan."
- "Anyone know the yen exchange rate? Our world tour starts tomorrow."
- "The hardest part of designing my guitar-shaped pool was deciding where to position the hot tub."

4. Overcome by curiosity, your target will ask who you are, and that's when you say, "I'm the bass player for Cheap Trick. A major rock band." If she doesn't believe you, model your patch for her. With any luck she'll reciprocate the favor, and you'll be out of that denim jacket before you know it.

VARIATIONS

Much like an actual rock star, you'll find you can perform slightly different versions of this number night after night with great success all over the world. Take a trip to Mumbai and you're the finger cymbalist for Ravi Shankar. Looking to get ljåid in Stockholm? Why not do so as Ace of Base's keytarist? In fact, Europe is probably the best place on earth to pose as a rock star. See The Hasselhoff.

CAUTION

While I always encourage a healthy injection of creativity while deceiving women, prudence dictates that you avoid the following musicians:

MUSICIAN	COMPLICATION
Led Zeppelin's drummer	RIP
anyone from Kiss	too easy/messy
Billy Idol	Ted already tried it and failed
Peter Frampton	voice difficult to emulate
Sting	reputation for tantric sex creates unrealistic endurance expectations

---

THE

BALLET DEFECTOR

Success Rate	7%
Attracts	dancer chicks, crazed capitalists
Requirements	unitard, believable Russian accent
Prep Time	forty-five minutes, or however long it takes to put on a unitard
Bummers	probably worked better in the 80s

☞ THE PLAY ☜

1. Build a time machine.

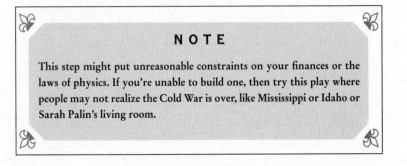

NOTE

This step might put unreasonable constraints on your finances or the laws of physics. If you're unable to build one, then try this play where people may not realize the Cold War is over, like Mississippi or Idaho or Sarah Palin's living room.

2. Unitard up!
3. Yes, you can stuff a tennis ball canister down there.

4. Approach your target and request political asylum in your best Russian accent. I'd suggest listening to the stand-up comedy of Yakov Smirnoff for practice except it's hard to hear when you're shoving a pair of scissors through your ear canal.
5. Tell your target you escaped from your touring ballet company but now you don't know what to do with all your grace, flexibility, and superhuman stamina.
6. If you can find your way out of the unitard, have sex with her.

THE

DOOGIE

Success Rate	20%
Attracts	fame hunters
Requirements	imagination
Prep Time	none!
Bummers	developing a sitcom is difficult

THE PLAY

1. Stare at your target until she looks back at you. Act annoyed and say, "Yes, yes, it's me, (your name)."
2. Off her quizzical look explain that you were a huge child star and you'd rather be known for who you are and not the character you played, even if he did make you millions of dollars.
3. When she asks what you starred in, offer some details from the chart of believable-sounding TV characters.
4. Now that she's enraptured by your fame, you can make your move.

CHART OF BELIEVABLE-SOUNDING TV CHARACTERS

Character	TV Show	Catchphrase
Stevie Judge	*Judge's Chambers*	"*You're* out of order!"
Richard P. Smedley III	*Nuclear Family*	"Does not compute."
Buddy Wemper	*Tiffany / Tiffany's Kids / The Wempers*	"Oopsie poopsie!"
Kyle Hooper ("The Hoop")	*Salad Days*	"Yeeeeeeeooooow!"
Danny Hill / Booraloo	*U.F. Uh-Oh*	"Here we go again." / "Flurblebutt zagooo!"

THE

ᴬU ᴾAIR

Success Rate	75%
Attracts	young foreign chicks
Requirements	a small collection of children's toys
Prep Time	a few hours
Bummers	shopping for children's toys can get competitive

☞ THE PLAY ☜

1. Acquire a few children's toys and strew them about your place.
2. Flip through magazines until you find a print ad featuring a kid. Cut it out and insert it into a picture frame. Repeat the process until you've got a few pictures of your "kid."

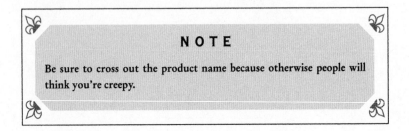

> ### N O T E
>
> Be sure to cross out the product name because otherwise people will think you're creepy.

3. Name your child, keeping in mind the latest fad is to steal one from a Jane Austen character for girls or use the last name of

a nineteenth-century president for boys. If even pretending to give your fake kid a pansy name like that makes you want to vomit, there's never any shame in "Junior."

4. Advertise in your local paper or online that you're looking for an au pair for your young child. Be sure to list requirements like previous experience, references, and CPR certification so that it looks legitimate. Oh, try to slip "big rack" somewhere in there too.

5. Invite prospective nannies over to your place to interview them and prominently display your pictures and kiddie toys. Explain that your child is at a lesson right now so you can really focus on getting to know her better. Since most au pairs wind up sleeping with the father anyway, maybe you'll find a go-getter who wants to get a head start.

THE

LOTTERY

Success Rate	45%
Attracts	money hounds
Requirements	lottery ticket, videocassette
Prep Time	an hour
Bummers	ironically expensive

THE PLAY

1. Videotape the lottery pick from your local television broadcast and buy a lottery ticket using the same numbers the following day.

2. Head to your local bar and bribe the bartender to play the recording. Don't offer more than twenty dollars since your chances of winning the lottery are about as good as winning the lottery.

3. Stand next to your target, signal the bartender to cue up the tape, and pull out your ticket. Help your cause by showing her the ticket while saying: "Here's to Rover's bone marrow transplant" or something equally as clever.

4. When the numbers are announced, start to hyperventilate and ask her to double-check your ticket. When she realizes it's a match, start to freak out. With any luck she'll be excited too and jump up and down, which is an added boobie bonus.

5. In the middle of the euphoria suddenly act worried and recite the following:

    "Great, now I'll be surrounded by people and women who only want me for my money. But you . . . you were talking to me before! Would you have dinner with me and help me figure out what to do with all this money?"

6. At dinner talk about all the charities you want to give to (see list below). Don't worry about paying for dinner: when the check comes, "discover" that you spent all your cash on the lottery ticket and, while chuckling, promise to pay her back.

7. Have sex with her.

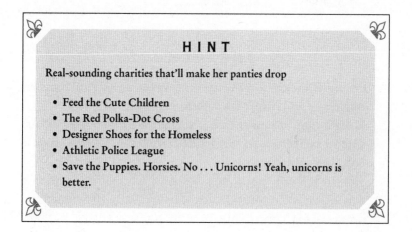

HINT

Real-sounding charities that'll make her panties drop

- Feed the Cute Children
- The Red Polka-Dot Cross
- Designer Shoes for the Homeless
- Athletic Police League
- Save the Puppies. Horsies. No . . . Unicorns! Yeah, unicorns is better.

THE

$\mathcal{C}$ALL $\mathcal{B}$ARNEY $\mathcal{S}$TINSON

Success Rate	99%
Attracts	star lovers
Requirements	good seats at a major sporting event
Prep Time	one hour
Bummers	astronomical wireless bill

THE PLAY

1. Obtain tickets to a major sporting event or another program featuring a giant television audience.
2. Make a sign addressed to hot single chicks with your phone number on it and wave it around like your sex life depends on it because it probably does.
3. Women will call, mistaking you for a celebrity despite the fact you displayed no particular talent or ability on television. Hey, it worked for Mario Lopez.
4. Try to convince callers to send you a picture so you don't waste your time setting up dates with ugmos or chicks who've been twenty-nine since Saddam Hussein was in power.
5. Have sex with your fans.

THE

Missing Cat

Success Rate	50%
Attracts	animal lovers
Requirements	a small travel crate
Prep Time	hours
Bummers	sneezing and scratching

THE PLAY

1. Take a stroll around the neighborhood paying particular mind to any and all lamppost flyers. Amid the ads for yard sales, open houses, and drum lessons, you're bound to find a flyer for a missing cat. Grab it.

2. Visit a local shelter and adopt a cat that looks pretty much like the missing cat.

   Q: *Is painting spots or stripes on the cat to match the missing one inhumane?*

   A: That's between you and your God.

3. Call the owner and deliver her "cat." If the owner's hot enough, collect your reward.

WHY DOES THIS WORK?

Science has revealed that 83% of cat owners are female while 100% are lonely.

THE

ᴛɪᴍᴇ ᴛʀᴀᴠᴇʟᴇʀ

Success Rate	1.21%
Attracts	sci-fi chicks, gullible gals
Requirements	old-man makeup, two bros
Prep Time	a good hour
Bummers	1.21% success rate

☞ THE PLAY ☜

1. Apply makeup so that you look like an old man. Feel free to go a little nuts with the varicose veins but not like Emperor Palpatine nuts.

2. Enter your local bar as an old man, approach a target, and ask for her name. After she offers it say, "I knew it. You're the (her name) who can change everything . . . or spell our inevitable doom."

3. Explain that you're on an urgent mission from the future. To prove it, point to one of your bros and say, loudly, that in exactly four seconds he's going to slap that guy, and then point to your less favorite bro.

4. That's the cue for your bro to slap the crap out of your other bro. It's best not to explain the plan to the third bro beforehand because

   A. he might object.
   B. it's way funnier when he doesn't see it coming.

5. Say that in a few minutes the young you from her time is going to enter and even though it might sound insane, in order to save the planet she needs to sleep with him. Tonight. In whatever way he wants. If she doesn't, he won't be able to find the solution to global warming that saves the human race.

6. Make your exit before she has time to poke any holes in the logic (don't worry, there aren't any). Say you've got to get back to the reality accelerator before the vortex closes or something sciencey like that to confuse her. Chicks do *not* understand science—that's just science.

7. Remove your old-man makeup, reenter the bar, and wait for her to identify you. If she's slow on the uptake—and she will be if this play has any chance of success—announce to nobody in particular that your top secret research project is really stressing you out.

8. Warm her globe.

THE

VAMPIRE

Success Rate	pretty high, I would guess
Attracts	chicks who think they're still fourteen
Requirements	Freshmint Tic Tacs, Scotch tape
Prep Time	however long it takes to tape Tic Tacs to your teeth to make fangs
Bummers	dressing goth

THE PLAY

1. Tell your target you're a vampire.
2. Have sex.

I realize this play is a little ill-formed, but vampires are hot right now, so it might work. Maybe you're like a vampire who has his own cooking show or custom cake shop? Those are also super en vogue. You could call your cake shop the Sweet Tooth. And on your business card, the little logo is a vampire's fangs biting into a designer cupcake. Hey, that'd actually be pretty cute! Um, I mean stupid. It'd be stupid. I don't care. Do it or don't do it, I really don't care. It was just a thought. Just chill out, man. Geez.

THE

BARNEY IDENTITY

Success Rate	13%, 74% if you look like Matt Damon
Attracts	paranoid types
Requirements	a fancy-looking pen
Prep Time	none
Bummers	too much running

THE PLAY

1. Once you've chosen your target, sprint up to her, hand her the pen, and recite the following lines: "Quick! Hide this in your bra. It's classified microfilm that might jeopardize our national security."
2. Take a good hard look to make sure she's hidden it well, then sprint out the door.
3. Return twenty minutes later with a little bit of a sweat going. (I'm hopeful you can think of a physical activity to occupy yourself with during that twenty minutes after peeking down her shirt.)
4. Tell her you've both got to get out of there: they're looking for you. You need to go someplace safe to defuse the pen bomb (she'll forget that you said microfilm earlier) but you can't go to your place because that's the first place they'll look.
5. Back at her place carefully unclick the pen and then exhale. Tell her she not only saved your life but the lives of your fellow Americans or whatever nationality you are . . . unless you're Russian, because then you're the bad guy. Sorry!
6. Enjoy having "we saved the world" sex.

THE

Young Man and the Sea

Success Rate	depends on whether they're biting or not
Attracts	naughty nauticals
Requirements	dirty sweater, winter cap, peg leg
Prep Time	a few days
Bummers	learning to tie knots

THE PLAY

1. Don't shave for a few days so your stubble grows out. If you're not a particularly hirsute fellow, a little stippling with a Sharpie can create the same effect.
2. Throw on a winter cap, a dirty sweater, and a world-weary scowl and hit up your local bar.
3. Set up camp next to your target and—to no one in particular—start talking about the dangers of life at sea. Some key terms that can help legitimize you are "rogue waves," "international shipping lanes," and "ghost pirates."
4. When your target finally asks what you do, say that you're a fisherman and you're headed to the high seas tomorrow for several months.

5. Once she takes the bait, you can lure her back to your place and give her the hook. Just to be crystal clear: I'm talking about sex.

WHY DOES THIS WORK?

At a primal level women like a man who can catch dinner using only his hands (and millions of dollars of trawling equipment, nets, sonar, etc.). They also like a man who laughs in the face of danger. A fisherman hits on both of these turn-ons, while his heading out to sea minimizes the chance of her friends discovering she got her ho on.

PLAYS FOR THE ADVANCED

(DON JUAN)

THE

PROJECT X

Success Rate	22–83% depending on cuteness of monkey
Attracts	animal lovers
Requirements	one chimpanzee, one chimpanzee leash
Prep Time	varies due to monkey availability
Bummers	play does *not* entail

- dressing chimp in a tuxedo
- dressing chimp in a baseball uniform
- dressing chimp in a tweed cape and deerstalker cap and having him smoke a pipe like he's Sherlock Holmes

THE PLAY

1. Get a monkey.
2. Take your monkey to a local bar.
3. Position yourself and your monkey near the target.
4. When she asks about your monkey, explain that you broke him out of an animal testing facility. If she presses, just shake your head and mutter, "Cosmetics."
5. Complain that you can't go home because "they" will be looking for you. She'll take the hint and invite you back to her place. If she hesitates, lie and assure her that the monkey is housebroken.
6. Slip the monkey some Benadryl so he won't be a distraction while you're getting it on with your target.

THE

LIFEGUARD

Success Rate	11%
Attracts	beach bunnies, college chicks
Requirements	sunscreen, a bro you trust
Prep Time	none!
Bummers	• might wind up with a dude resuscitating you • might look a little stupid • might die

THE PLAY

1. Identify a lifeguard babe at a pool or beach.
2. Get in the water, put your face down, and stop breathing.
3. If you're brought back to life, it'll hopefully be at the lips of the hot chick.
4. If she saves your life, insist on taking her to dinner. Adrenaline over the day's events should carry you to the bedroom, where your trusted bro can film the whole thing.

NOTE

While the entire play hinges on her bringing you back to life, you should be aware that hot chick lifeguards are not traditionally hired for their CPR or other life-saving skills. They're hired because they look good in a swimsuit with a whistle between their boobs. If she doesn't revive you, then your trusted bro can, though it should be noted that he can't be blamed—even from the afterlife—if he fails to do so because he's checking out the lifeguard babe because she looks good in a swimsuit with a whistle between her boobs.

THE

DIET GURU

Success Rate	50%
Attracts	chicks with body image issues, aka all of them: thanks, Barbie!
Requirements	relatively trim physique
Prep Time	none!
Bummers	talking about food makes you hungry

THE PLAY

1. Approach your target and compliment her on how fit she is. Ask her what she eats, then immediately apologize: you're just curious because you're a doctor who created your own miracle diet. Yep, you devised a way to eat whatever you want and still stay slim. Even an entire pint of fudge ripple? Even an entire pint of fudge ripple.

2. Drunk on the idea that you hold the key to effortless weight loss, your target will inquire about your program. Tell her you can show her how it works but you'll need to see the contents of her refrigerator first.

3. Back at her place explain how she can eat whatever she wants as long as she frenetically exercises at the same time.

4. Explain the ins and outs of your plan over some frenetic ins and outs.

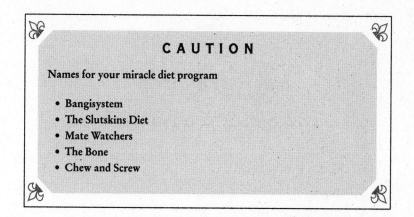

C A U T I O N

Names for your miracle diet program

- Bangisystem
- The Slutskins Diet
- Mate Watchers
- The Bone
- Chew and Screw

THE

DÉJÀ VU

Success Rate	30% 30%
Attracts	gullible gals
Requirements	a bro you can count on to screw up
Prep Time	a few beers
Bummers	"A bro you can count on to screw up might screw up by not screwing up." Confucius

THE PLAY

1. Have a wingman choose a play from the book and run it poorly on your target.
2. After he swings and misses, approach the target and run the same play.
3. When she freaks out and says your wingman just tried to run that play, sell him out. Explain that he's trying to capitalize on your life: you're the real bassist for Cheap Trick or the real Jorge Posada or whatever.
4. After you bond over what a creep your wingman is, it's just a hop, skip, and a jump to Laidville.

THE

FALL IN LOVE

Success Rate	95%
Attracts	all types
Requirements	patience, open ear, open heart
Prep Time	a few months to a year
Bummers	very time-consuming, can be expensive

THE PLAY

1. Approach your target and introduce yourself.
2. Make casual conversation and exchange information so you can meet up at a later date.
3. Over the course of anywhere from a couple weeks to a few months, endeavor to find out what interests and values you have in common. At the same time try to learn what particular observations and gestures make her laugh and smile.
4. As you become increasingly intimate, you might find yourself thinking about her at odd times or buying something for her just because you know she'll laugh at how stupid it is. That's perfectly okay.
5. Now that you're in love, you can bang her and move on to the next conquest!

THE
I Can Land This Plane

Success Rate	9%
Attracts	nervous flyers
Requirements	two first-class tickets, makeup, turbulence
Prep Time	none
Bummers	• costly • have to sit in coach for part of the flight • air travel a mess these days

THE PLAY

1. Buy two first-class tickets on the same flight.
2. Board the plane, sit in one of your seats, and examine the talent as it parades down the aisle in front of you. You might want to cut a couple of eyeholes in your newspaper so you don't get caught.
3. Before takeoff walk down the aisle until you find your target. Quietly offer the person sitting next to her your first-class seat. If you need a reason, say the seat is your lucky number or the person won a contest or you want to sit with commoners for a change.
4. At the first hint of turbulence look out the window and say, "Oh my God, we just lost the camel strut valve."
5. Explain that you're an off-duty pilot and that losing the camel strut valve is a serious issue. How serious? You landed a plane

114

in this condition once in a simulator but it's never been done in real life. The pilots need your help. We all do.

6. March toward the front of the plane and sit in your other first-class seat for the remainder of the flight. Right before landing, apply some bruise makeup and splash some water on your face as if you've been sweating.

7. After landing stand at the front and nod appreciatively as if the passengers are thanking you. When your target approaches, exit with her and see if you can land that plane too.

THE

$\mathcal{B}$OY IN THE $\mathcal{B}$UBBLE

Success Rate	1%, but a fun 1%
Attracts	dummies
Requirements	a giant bubble
Prep Time	about an hour to inflate giant bubble
Bummers	can get hot inside giant bubble

THE PLAY

1. Acquire a giant bubble.
2. Get inside the giant bubble.
3. Head to your local bar in the giant bubble.
4. Tell your target that you're confined to life inside the giant bubble and that the worst part about living inside a giant bubble is never knowing the touch of a woman.
5. "Accidentally" open the giant bubble and make contact with her arm. When you don't die immediately, freak out and thank her for curing you.
6. Later invite her inside your giant bubble for some giant bubble sex.

THE

MRS. STINSFIRE

Success Rate	7%
Attracts	college chicks
Requirements	fat suit, old-lady makeup, pince-nez spectacles . . . maybe some fake pearls?
Prep Time	one semester
Bummers	sorority rush procedures confusing

THE PLAY

1. Search college websites until you find a job listing for a sorority housemom. It might take several weeks to a lifetime but it'll be worth it.

2. Dress up like an old lady. Think Barbara Bush, Betty White, or present-day Rod Stewart.

3. Once you get the job, introduce yourself to "your girls" and immediately start talking up your wealthy son.

4. Convince the chapter to invest in a high-tech security system complete with a closed-circuit video surveillance package—you know, for safety.

5. Have your "son" come to visit one weekend, suddenly take ill and retreat to your room, and set "him" loose.

WARNING!

To avoid getting immediately fired, you'll be expected to fulfill the duties of housemom. To get started, consult the following suggested activities calendar.

SAMPLE SORORITY CALENDAR

	Monday	Tuesday	Wednesday	Thursday	Friday	Saturday	Sunday
8 pm	Rush tea	*Skit nite!* Topic: "Your body and you"	Seniors: resumes and cover letters Underclassmen: kissing contest!	Visiting lecturer Professor Dorothy Williams: "The Feminist Struggle"	Chapter portrait! Theme? *Wild animals… Rawwwrrr!*	*Spring formal!*	Movie night! *Legally Blonde* *Barely Legally Blonde*
9 pm		Chapter meeting *Pillow fight!*	Leadership council	First annual bikini kitchen clean	Panty exchange party	*Spring formal!*	*Die Hard*
10 pm	Bed check	Bed check	Shower check	Bed check			

119

THE

BOUNCER

Success Rate	30%, 3% in the rain
Attracts	exclusive chicks
Requirements	boom box, velvet ropes, clipboard
Prep Time	a few hours
Bummers	scoring with your target not as awesome as watching your favorite artist live

THE PLAY

1. Suit up.
2. Find a back or side door in a location where a lot of potential targets walk by and create a boundary around it using velvet ropes and stanchions.

   Q: *Where can I get velvet ropes and stanchions?*
   A: They are readily available at your local movie theater or museum. Just go and take them. If anybody asks what you're doing, point to your clipboard, shrug, and say, "Maintenance."

3. Choose a live album featuring your favorite (living) recording artist and load it up in the boom box. Hit play and then "guard" the door.

4. People will start lining up because nothing attracts people more than other people standing in line . . . especially when you're there telling them Bruce Springsteen is playing a private concert inside and maybe you'll let them in.

5. Choose a target from the line, find out how desperately she wants to get inside, and see if you can work out an "arrangement."

THE

BILLIONAIRE

Success Rate	100%
Attracts	any woman throughout space and time
Requirements	$1,000,000,000.00
Prep Time	most likely several lifetimes
Bummers	• tax rates • signing giant checks for charities leads to serious hand crampage • mega yacht takes so long to build, when you finally finish, it's already obsolete, ugh!

☞ THE PLAY ☜

1. Accumulate a billion dollars.

2. Sleep with women.

THE

TROJAN LESBIAN

Success Rate	< 1%
Attracts	lesbians, experimental chicks
Requirements	luck
Prep Time	forty-five minutes
Bummers	adjusting to discrimination

THE PLAY

1. Dress as you think a lesbian would dress. Since there isn't a dress code, anything you choose will inevitably be offensive but it's the only way this play gets off the ground.
2. Shave as closely as you can. Your face, I mean.
3. Hit up a gay bar and approach the hottest chick you can find. After you make sure she's Adam's apple–free, ask if she wants to get out of there.
4. Later, when you're fooling around, try to hide your maleness as long as possible. If and when the cat gets out of the bag, do your best to convince her it's synthetic. Try not to snap when she wonders why you'd buy such a small one.

THE

FOOTLOOSE

Success Rate	100%
Attracts	backward townspeople
Requirements	dance moves, flour mill, backward town
Prep Time	travel to backward town
Bummers	backward town

THE PLAY

1. See if any towns around you have banned dancing and/or rock music. If you can't find one, catch a bus to a prairie state. Or Utah.
2. Once you've found a devil-weary community, start blasting rock-and-roll hits from the likes of Kenny Loggins while working on your dance moves in an empty flour mill. This will somehow anger the locals and, more important, turn on all the repressed country babes.
3. Win a chicken race on a tractor.
4. Organize a town dance where you can have your pick of the local ladies.

THE

GRIEVING CHICKS

Success Rate	wish it were 0%
Attracts	bereft chicks, an eternity of guilt
Requirements	zero integrity
Prep Time	none . . . if you have no soul
Bummers	• hospital smell • hospital food • hospital magazine selection

☛ THE PLAY ☚

1. Hang out in a hospital waiting room.
2. Choose a target from among the gathered friends and family.
3. When and if a doctor delivers bad news, offer her your shoulder and other body parts to cry on.
4. Donate lots of money to the hospital or something because, buddy, that was cold.

Q: *Um, aren't you the one who published the play?*
A: Shut up.

THE

E PLURIBUS UNUM

Success Rate	28%
Attracts	destiny girls
Requirements	patience
Prep Time	years
Bummers	hand cramps

THE PLAY

1. Choose a target.
2. Write your name and number on a dollar bill and give it to her. Tell her to spend it—but make her promise to call you if she ever gets it back, because then the universe is clearly telling you to be together.
3. Go to your bank, withdraw five thousand dollars in singles, and write your name and number on all of them.
4. Repeat steps 1 and 2 until you've circulated all your bills, and get ready for those phone calls.

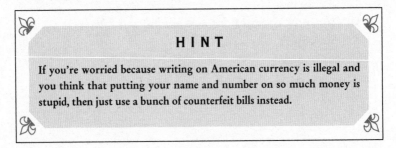

HINT

If you're worried because writing on American currency is illegal and you think that putting your name and number on so much money is stupid, then just use a bunch of counterfeit bills instead.

127

THE

MR. PRESIDENT

Success Rate	.0000000001%
Attracts	Beltway babes, voters
Requirements	firm handshake, white teeth, 270 electoral votes
Prep Time	at least thirty-five years
Bummers	• kissing babies • appearing faithful • campaigning is a real bear

THE PLAY

1. Win a local office and skyrocket to state representative by opposing the incumbent closest to death.
2. Become governor and cling to a primarily populist agenda but throw a little pork to the fat cats by luring at least one major corporation into the state. Balance yourself politically by taking a hard-line stance on the death penalty while quietly cutting funding for executions. If the economy is up, take credit. If the economy is down, blame the legislature or, if you're in a border state, illegal immigrants.
3. After two terms begin campaigning for president. Generate a progressive platform that panders to your party's extremes but can seamlessly convert to a more centrist stance after the primaries. Sink your money into Iowa and New Hampshire, make an

appearance in South Carolina and Nevada, and set up camp in Missouri and New Jersey if you still need Super Tuesday to win the nomination.

4. If you're not from the South, choose a running mate who is. It's also time to pick a theme song. Anything by Fleetwood Mac will do as long as it's not "Little Lies," "Landslide," or "Rhiannon" because that would just be weird.

5. Visit a military base, throw out a first pitch without bouncing it over the plate, and do at least one photo shoot where you're wearing a construction helmet. Promise to run a clean campaign but have your running mate take potshots at the opponent with patronizingly down-home colloquialisms like "that's not how we run things on the farm" or "that's not the Main Street I know" or "where I'm from that's called cooking your grits before the gamecock warbles."

6. Win an absolute majority of electoral votes or a Supreme Court runoff and confidently yet solemnly take the oath of office—this is a serious responsibility.

7. Start banging chicks.

WHY DOES THIS WORK?

Women are drawn to power and you can't get more powerful than the president without owning a major media conglomerate. While we all think of Kennedy and Clinton as the preeminent Oval Office lotharios, it was Franklin Roosevelt who really exploited the position. Not only did he feign polio and confine himself to a wheelchair in order to generate a "wounded bird" attraction to complement his commander-in-chief allure, but he was also the only president to serve more than two terms. The country hadn't seen that sort of commitment to booty since James "Poke" Polk.

THE

KIDNEY SCHEME

Success Rate	24%
Attracts	big-hearted chicks who are hopefully also big-breasted chicks
Requirements	hospital bracelet, bro
Prep Time	minimal
Bummers	have to know what the kidney does

THE PLAY

1. Put on a hospital bracelet. If you don't have one, root around inside a hospital dumpster. You're bound to pick one up ... among other things.
2. Once you've identified your target, flash your arm until she notices the bracelet. Say you don't want to talk about it and then immediately explain that you just gave one of your kidneys to your buddy. Wave to your bro and have him wave back.

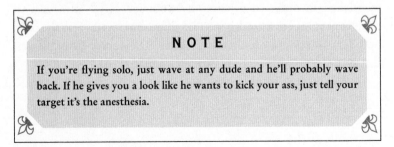

NOTE

If you're flying solo, just wave at any dude and he'll probably wave back. If he gives you a look like he wants to kick your ass, just tell your target it's the anesthesia.

3. Tell her you've been best friends since grade school and if he didn't make it, well ... let's just say it was a no-brainer to kidney-five him. If you can choke back a few tears here, that will lubricate matters. Speaking of which ...
4. After you assure her that your remaining organs are in perfect working order, it's time to suggest making another donation ...

THE

I Can Guess Your Weight

Success Rate	65%
Attracts	all women
Requirements	basic math
Prep Time	none!
Bummers	miscalculations can get ugly

THE PLAY

1. Approach your target and announce that you can guess her weight.
2. Intrigued, mortified, and paralyzed by her body-image issues, she'll want to know your guess.
3. Take what you think she really weighs and subtract twenty-five pounds. Now subtract another five. Give her this number.
4. Have sex with her.

THE

HEIMLICH MANEUVER

Success Rate	5%
Attracts	EMT chicks
Requirements	pretzel
Prep Time	none!
Bummers	might accidentally choke to death

THE PLAY

1. Once you've chosen your target, pretend to choke on a pretzel in front of her.

2. After she performs the Heimlich or pats you on the back or even if she does absolutely nothing at all, spit out the pretzel and gasp for air. You can't go too big here.

3. Grab her hands and explain how, now that she's saved your life, you're honor bound to stay by her side forever.

4. Hover around until she can't take it anymore and tries to absolve you of the life debt. Tell her that won't work. The code of your people expressly states that you have to stay by her side until you save her life or she sleeps with you. Those are the rules.

5. Hopefully she goes for it. If not, well, you've always got what's left of your pretzel.

THE

$\mathcal{G}$HOST OF $\mathcal{C}$HRISTMAS $\mathcal{F}$UTURE

Success Rate	not good
Attracts	prudish types
Requirements	a day planner and a black cloak, like what the weirdest kid in your high school wore to picture day; must be performed on December 23
Prep Time	cloaking time
Bummers	overwhelming selection of day planners

THE PLAY

1. Put on your cloak and hood up.
2. Approach your target and say, "You've already met the other two ghosts. Now it's time to visit a Christmas yet to come."
3. Off her confusion pull out your day planner, smack yourself in the head, and say, "Oh man, I'm a day early. Daylight savings, prime meridian . . . what have you. My bad."
4. Pull back your hood and explain the deal: tomorrow two ghosts will appear and show her Christmases of the past and present. Beg her to act surprised, because if those two jokers find out about this, you'll never hear the end of it.
5. Curiosity will drive her to ask about her future. Be evasive and

say she'll find out tomorrow night, but when she demands to know, take a deep breath and tell her she's going to die alone because she doesn't have enough casual sex with strangers. There. You said it. You could get in so much trouble for this breach of protocol.

6. As she mulls over her lonely future, open your day planner and wonder aloud what you're going to do for the rest of the night. You're all dressed up with no one to haunt . . .

7. Scrooge her. (Yeah, I did. Come on, it was *right* there!)

THE

$CUBA $DIVER

Success Rate	1%
Attracts	chicks who think they can change dudes, so pretty much all of them
Requirements	oxygen tank, mask, flippers, wet suit, regular suit (for under the wet one)
Prep Time	a few years
Bummers	wet suit can cause skin rash

THE PLAY

1. Tell a meddlesome female friend about *The Playbook*.
2. Run a play on one of her coworkers, making her so angry she steals *The Playbook*.
3. Put on the scuba suit and tell your friend you're going to do one more scam called "The Scuba Diver" on the hot girl standing by the bar.
4. Your friend, let's call her Lily, goes and talks to the girl and tells her everything about *The Playbook*.
5. Lily and the target will demand to know how The Scuba Diver works. Take off your mask and give them some spiel about your deep-seated insecurities, which don't really exist because let's face it, you're awesome.

6. Now Lily will feel bad and talk you up to the target until she agrees to go get coffee with you.

7. And it. Is. On.

WARNING!

Be sure to rip these pages out before performing The Scuba Diver!

TROUBLESHOOTING
AND FAQS

Why do so many of the plays ask me to lie about who I am or what I can do, like in The My Penis Grants Wishes?
Whoa. It's not a lie. It's never a lie, okay? Maybe you were embellishing a little bit but you weren't lying. As far as all the embellishment goes, it's unfortunately par for the course on the sexual battlefield. Women have grossly embellished what they claim they expect from men. According to them men should do things like "call back" or "communicate" or "care." Since the only world where that's gonna happen is inhabited by leprechauns, unicorns, and Gypsies,* it's only fair that you're allowed to tell a woman you've been marooned on Earth and the only way for you to return to Andromeda is to have sexual intercourse with her . . . but it can't be like "lay-there-and-do-nothing" intercourse because that won't work, what with dark matter and wormholes and whatnot. Solar flares too. That's a good one to toss in there.

---

* Editor's note: Despite the preponderance of evidence, Barney refuses to accept that Gypsies are, in fact, a real people indigenous to Eastern Europe and *not* a "mythical, magical people who ride around in caravans putting jinxes on hot chicks."

Won't a woman become furious when she finds out later I was—cough—embellishing?

First of all, who cares? You are *looong* gone by then. Second, no! Women love clinging to a fantasy. They want to believe in a world where Santa Claus is real and vampires live for eternity but stop aging at a freshly postpubescent nineteen and that the president is actually elected by the people and not a secret cadre of businessmen who meet every three months in Aruba, though there's a movement to try a different island for the next meeting because even though it's Aruba, it's getting a little stale. If a woman wants so desperately to believe in all those things, then she'll readily buy that you're the heir to the Tootsie Roll fortune or the prince of Europia or a sensitive guy.

But what if I get caught in the middle of the play?

She'll love it! Above all else, women love attention. Of any kind. Remember, a woman is naturally attracted to a jerk. Why? Because her dad is one. He secretly wanted a boy and doesn't know how to connect with her, so he just ignores her. It'd be tragic if it didn't produce such a needy chick. In fact, it is my dream to one day send a giant fruit basket to all the terrible fathers who have created the legion of slutty daughters we all enjoy so much today. Thank you, crappy fathers.

Seriously, what if she doesn't love the fact that I'm just trying to sleep with her?

Okay. Look. Even if the play goes horribly awry and your target winds up getting mad and throwing her totally delish cosmo in your face, there's still a pretty decent chance one of her hot friends will pause in the middle of filling out the police report and think, "Hey, at least he put in the effort to meet a woman. Some guys just don't even care." Then maybe you can hook up with her later . . . if you have a good lawyer.

ABOUT THE AUTHORS

BARNEY STINSON has slept with countless women yet has never had a pregnancy scare he's legally aware of. When not explaining how to be awesome on his popular website, www.barneysblog.com, Barney enjoys modeling underwear; bottling one of his 83 wine labels; and being photographed with orphans, abandoned puppies, or anything that really sells "vulnerable" when accompanied by a Sarah McLachlan song.

MATT KUHN is a writer for the TV show *How I Met Your Mother*. In addition to producing Barney's Blog he has written five episodes for the show, including "Slapsgiving," "Three Days of Snow," and "Double Date." He has also written two other books in collaboration with Barney Stinson—*The Bro Code* and *Bro on the Go*. Matt lives in Los Angeles with his wife, Alecia, and their dog, Maggie, who, despite being full grown, is not taller than his knee—a clear violation of The Bro Code. Oops.